How to Get Rich

By Understanding the Economy

KYLE C.

ABOUT THIS BOOK

There are more lives being destroyed in recent years due to mismanagement of their financials. Many of those admitted that they spend more than they earn, resulting in deficits. As high as 80% of the people I know do not have a habit of keeping a spending journal or formulating a budget. A lot of them in fact are spending impulsively in this consumer product-centric era. The situation was made worse with the rising use of social media where every product is touted as a must-have by the "influencers". Without having those products, one might be looked down by his or her peers. Every year, we are being bombarded by millions of products. Just smartphones alone, there are hundreds of models being introduced each year. Even companies and countries are finding it difficult to manage their finance. This is due to the fact that there is an imbalance in money flow in the economy, resulting in a massive wealth gap among the people in society.

I hope that you have a good time reading this book and hope that the information in this book is able to assist you in your financial plan.

WHAT IS THE ECONOMY?

A lot of people have heard a lot of this term but do not exactly know what it is. We keep seeing it in the news that the economy is doing well, or the economic outlook is really bad and that companies or the common people are running out of money in a bad economy. Whenever there is an economic crisis, we will notice that the government will announce "stimulus packages" worth billions of dollars to pump in more money into the economy in order to prevent it from collapsing.

So, what is actually happening?

To put it in simple terms, the economy is formed when a movement of money or resources across different people or entities stemmed from the supply and demands of goods. Humans have evolved to a higher level of existence than animals where we have learnt to utilise the resources available around us and began exchanging goods between us in order to get the supplies we need. The world is not created equal, that is a fact. The same goes for the disbursement of the resources when Earth was formed. Certain areas will some resources that are not available elsewhere. Because of this, humans started to exchange goods among each other in the form of a barter system. This also facilitates the creation of jobs since we have our own strengths, weaknesses, passions, and dislikes. We would focus on doing something that we are good at, or we like. However, we do have common needs, but we do not have the time to acquire those goods for the need. The barter activities the start of the supply and demand cycle.

As civilisations became more advanced, we yearn for things that are not part of our basic needs. We are curious about new and fancy things, developing the urge to possess things that we might or might not need.

That is when we have the first market for trading. As the empire expands, the capital will become a central trading zone for merchants from all over the empire, including outside of the empire.

When the transactions happen, it will start to generate economic activities.

THE ECONOMIC MODEL

The economic model can be as small as comprising just a few individuals, or as large as the entire region. The term "economy" doesn't just apply specifically to a country. It can apply to an individual, a household, or a company. As a matter of fact, the origin of the word "economy" is derived from the Greek word "*oikonomia*", which can be translated to household management.

Trading activities are the key to driving the economy of an individual, company, or even a country. When trading activities happens, goods exchange will take place. However, as the population grows, businesses expand. Demand increases tremendously. The effort to bring all your wares to be exchanged at the market soon became impossible. Imagine a golden goblet is worth thirty cattle. If you are a wealthy farm owner that wishes to get your hands on the goblet so you may showcase your wealth to your neighbour, you will need to transport all thirty cattle to the market just to exchange for the goblet. To overcome this issue, humans began to use other items that hold value, and small enough to carry in large quantities to exchange for goods. Thus, the concept of money was born and became the standard of measurement and the converter for one to purchase a specific good or service. Gold, silver, or any precious metals were most widely used as money back in the old days. When those metal became too troublesome or unsafe to carry around, paper currency was developed by the Chinese to alleviate the burden.

The Chinese have mastered the art of trade centuries back. They understood the fundamentals of the economy and were, still is, obsess about making more money. There is a Chinese saying,

Money = Water

The Chinese always equate money with the flow of water. You will find water features and fountains incorporated in many building designs according to *Fengshui*. In fact, the term *Fengshui* is translated to "Wind-Water", which shows the importance of the water element in the Chinese belief system. The flow of water represents the flow of money in an economy. The water features in a *Fengshui* design will always be built in such a way where the water is flowing to the owner of the premise. It signifies that money will continue to flow to their business consistently.

The following illustrates how an economic model is described using the flow of water in a tank system.

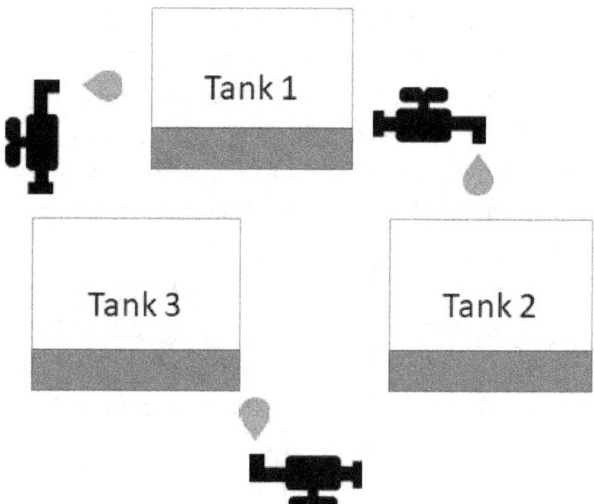

There are three identical tanks, each with a water tap attached to it. To ensure that every tank will never run dry and they get the same amount of water in the tank, the water is set to flow consistently from one tank to another tank. In this way, every tank will have the same amount of water at all times. This would be the ideal condition in the economy where everyone will be able to have an equal amount of resources.

However, we live in an imperfect world. Reality is harsh and brutal. There is no such thing as equality in this world as every individual is made different and has different qualities. We think differently. Everyone is for themselves. Some might be stingy; some might be greedier than the rest. With different personal agendas in mind, people will behave differently. Because of this, a person will limit the water flow to the next tank so that he will be able to accumulate more water for other users. This will cause a discrepancy in the water levels between the water tanks since tank 1 is receiving more than it is giving out.

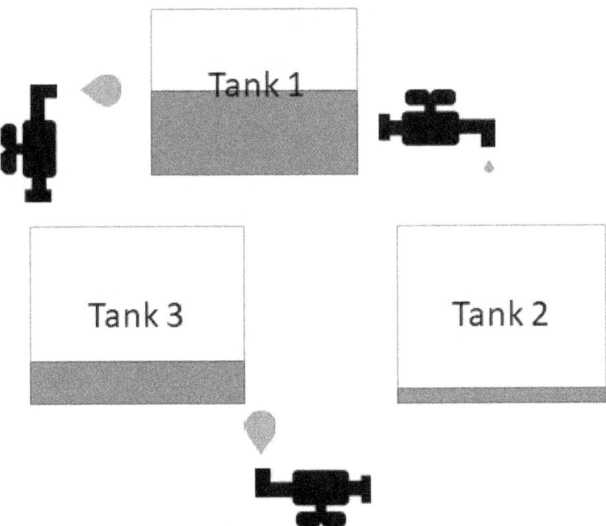

Under this setup, the person running Tank 1 will have more water than the other two, making him the "richest" in terms of water volume he has, followed by Tank 3 and Tank 2. This is exactly what causes some people to have more money than others through excessive saving.

However, the model above is not sustainable and it will cause severe problems to the "economy" of the three tanks above. If the person running Tank 1 continues to limit the amount of water to Tank 2, ultimately Tank 2 will run dry. With that, Tank 3 will not be able to receive adequate water from Tank 3 and will end up with a dry tank as well. In return, the incoming flow from Tank 3 to Tank 1 will eventually stop as well.

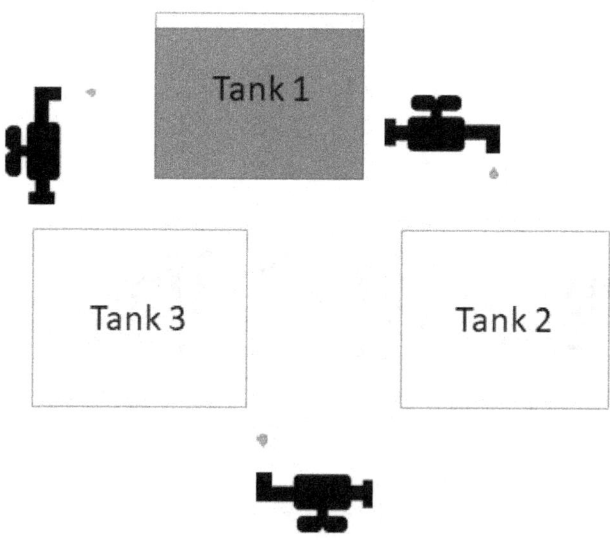

With Tank 2 and Tank 3 dried up, the water flow stops. Tank 2 and Tank 3 will be rendered useless. Those who rely on the two tanks for the water source will be greatly affected. They will have no other choice but to severely limit the use of the remaining water. When there are none, they will be doomed.

This is what causes bankruptcies and layoffs in reality when an individual or a company runs out of money.

How to fix this situation?

The ideal solution would be Tank 1 releasing back the water to Tank 2 so that it can be filled up and supply the water to Tank 3. With that, the situation will go back to its initial state where the water can be distributed evenly to all the water tanks.

What if Tank 1 is still a stingy, greedy bastard?

If Tank 1 refused to release more water to Tank 2, then one alternative solution for Tank 2 would be sourcing from another water source to prevent it from being dried up.

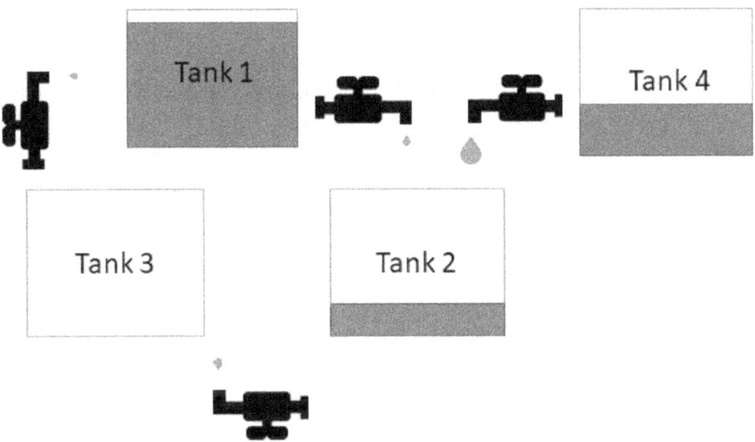

With the new water source, this could revive Tank 2 and provide the required water to Tank 3. However, depending on the terms and conditions set by the operator from Tank 4, it could bring more harm than good in the long run. If the Tank 4 operator is channeling more water into Tank 2 with no conditions, then the economy will continue to run without issues, only with Tank 1 running the risk of being overflowed.

But what if Tank 4 requested Tank 2 to pay back the water with an extra 20% of the volume that was given out?

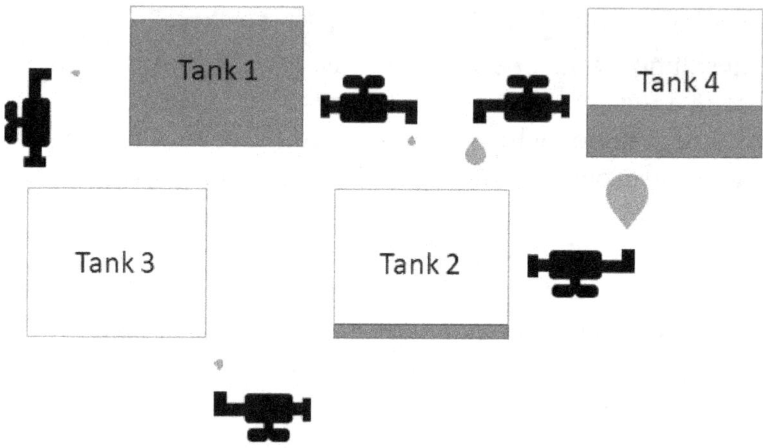

Tank 2 will be running out of water pretty soon if the supply from Tank 1 could not be used to cover the extra volume required by Tank 4. The whole water flow would grind to a halt again when Tank 2 is empty. It will only run again if either Tank 1 or Tank 4 increases the flow of water to the system, or Tank 2 sources its water from other places, which runs into the same risk as it does with Tank 4.

Sounds familiar? Look at your loans.

The global economy model becomes complicated a gazillion fold if you add the total of the human populations, all the companies, and all the trading activities that are happening around the world.

HOW TO GET RICH?

After understanding the basic economy, how can utilise the knowledge to make more money?

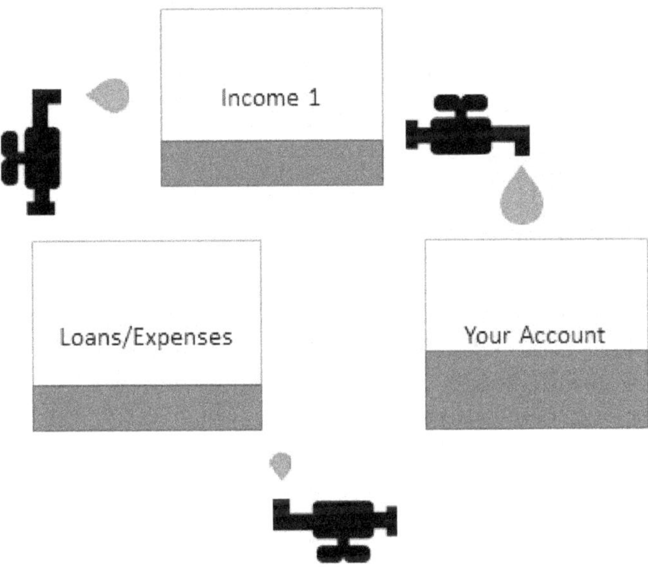

The first step to ensure that you have more dough in your bank account is plain old simple math:

$$Income > Expenses$$

The income that you get from your job must be greater than your expenses. With the extra cash, one could save it in the high-interest saving accounts, or place them in other investment vehicles to generate more income. Nowadays, with consumer-centric products and the influence of social media, more and more people are spending more than they could afford. One does not need to change his or her phone every year. The only thing that these people buy expensive things that they can barely afford is to showcase them on their social media, just so that their friends could get jealous.

The low barrier of getting credit cards from banks only added more fuel to the fire. According to statistics, a staggering amount of bankruptcies filed in the country was due to credit card debts. When a person is swiping their credit card happily on the machine, he or she is effectively spending future money. This situation changes the equation above where one must always be sure that they never overspend. Through the convenience of a credit card, the equation has changed to

$$\text{Income} - \text{credit card debt} < \text{Expenses}$$

The income of the individual will be greatly reduced as one will need to pay off the credit card debt the following month. Things got exponentially worse if the cardholder was unable to pay off the debt. The insane interest rate imposed on the credit card for late or non-payment, with its compounding effect will snowball into a gigantic debt that the cardholder will no longer have the ability to pay back.

The feeling of splashing out always feels great, but temporary. It is the same as taking drugs. You will feel great momentarily, but the consequences can be devastating.

Remember,

Only use future money for emergencies

"Wants are different from needs."

"Feed our brains, not our egos."

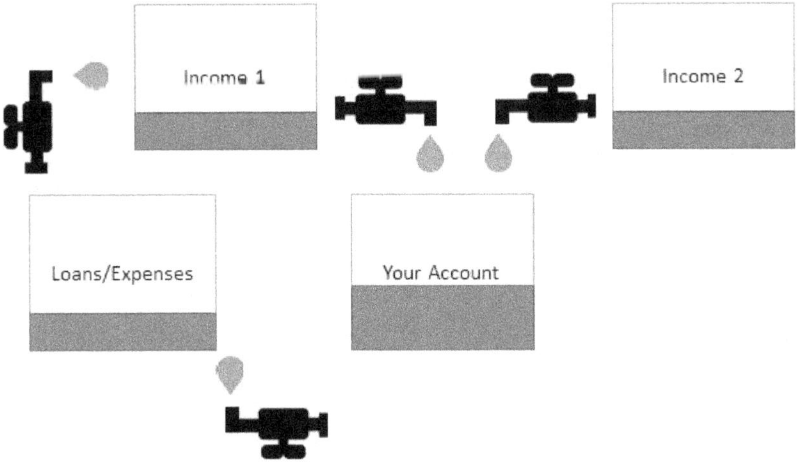

The second step is to ensure that you have multiple forms of income, not expenses. Try cutting down the expenses for things that are non-essential, e.g. weekly dinner at some fancy restaurants, the daily dose of coffee from the famous coffee chains, upgrading your phone to a newer model every year, so on and so forth.

Budget preparation

It is a good habit to formulate a budget for your expenses. This is to ensure that you are always able to keep track of where your money is wasted, I mean spent. You are also able to make adjustments to your expenditure whenever required, e.g. economic slowdown, or cut down unnecessary spending.

All you need is a pen and paper. If you are tech-savvy, you could do it on the spreadsheet or any free mobile apps out there.

Step 1:

Prepare a budget and list down all your current expenses:

Income	USD per month
Salary	3,200.00
Expenses	
Coffee	400.00
Dinner	600.00
Fuel	500.00
Bills	500.00
Entertainment	500.00
Rental	500.00
Balance	200.00

Step 2:

Cut down or reduce unnecessary expenses so that you will end up with a bigger balance.

Income	USD per month
Salary	3,200.00
Expenses	
Coffee	100.00
Dinner	200.00
Fuel	500.00
Bills	200.00
Entertainment	100.00
Rental	500.00
Balance	1,600.00

Step 3:

Use the added cash at hand for other investments, or save up in the high interest fixed deposit accounts.

Balance	USD per month
Salary	1,600.00
Investments	
Savings account at 3% per annum	600.00
Stocks	500.00
Bonds	500.00

Step 4:

Use the extra money generated from the investments or interests received from your saving account and increase the amount in those investments.

Step 5:

Repeat step 4.

If you have extra time at hand or special skills, you could try to increase your passive or active income types.

Active Income	Passive Income
Second Job	Renting out extra rooms or properties

Selling things	Stock Investments
Freelance work	Interests from High Yield Savings account
	Royalties from books

Definitions:

- **Active income** - This will take up a sizeable chunk of your time in order to maintain the business. If you stop, the income stops.

- **Passive income** – You will still get paid without working once you have already set up or have invested in them. The income will be a recurring occurrence until the business or the investment went bust. You can earn money even when you sleep.

It is recommended to increase the passive income over time so that you will have more money sources for your other job or investment. Remember the multiple water source model? This will be the setup that you would want to go for if you planning to have more money in your bank account.

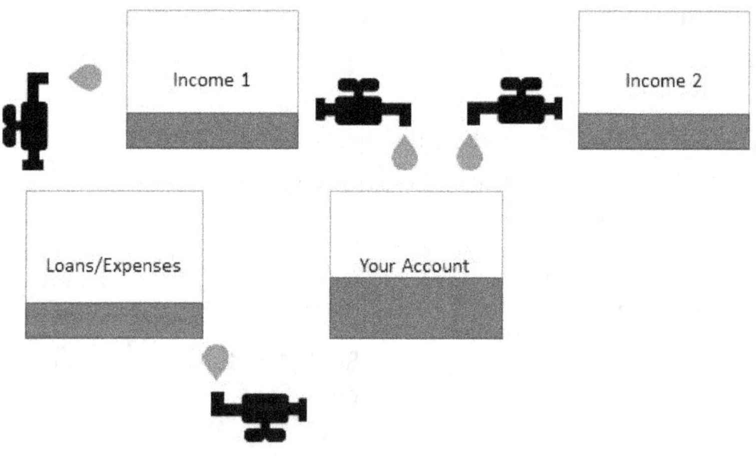

The diagram above illustrates the income setup where most people should establish if they want to achieve financial freedom or becoming rich. The person must have multiple income sources that will help to provide continuous income streams to support their life should one loses his or her job during the economic downtimes. The extra revenue stream will help to alleviate some burden while he or she looks for a new job. The extra money also comes in handy if one decides to start his or her businesses. One way to quickly set up a new income stream without putting too much effort until it disrupts our main job is through investments.

Imagine your stock investment generates 1,000 dollars from the dividends every month. You now have 4,200 dollars of income in total. (3,200 from the main job)

If you reinvest the money to purchase more stocks, you will increase your income to 1,500 dollars from investments. Repeated the process so that your passive income will surpass your main income. Assuming that the dividend is paid out consistently, you would be able to achieve financial freedom.

When we talk about investments, we often hear others saying "one should always invest in good assets" to generate returns.

WHAT IS AN ASSET?

An asset is a piece of item that holds value and may or may not generate passive income for the owner. Examples of assets are stocks, properties, commodities, and collectibles.

A good asset retains its value e.g. properties or gold. When the resource became scarce and the demand for it increases, its value will increase as people will be competing at higher prices to own it.

A bad asset loses its value over time, e.g. a car or gadgets like smartphones and laptops. Stocks of companies with huge debts or properties that are unfavourable are also considered as bad assets since they would not fetch good value and one might lose more money than the returns for owning them.

Therefore, it is in the best interest to invest in good assets to maximise the return. You should study the value of an asset before making the purchase. Every asset or goods hold value by itself. The supply and demand factor will influence its value.

How can one know the value of an asset for investment?

I have discussed a lot on how one can determine the value of an asset or investment in my other book, *Layman's Guide to Investing, with a bit of common sense (2020), by Kyle C*. I highly recommend you to check it out.

Is money considered an asset?

Contrary to what most people think, modern currency is not considered an asset as the actual worth of the money is actually the cost of that paper. Yes, currency or paper money is worthless. The paper money is just a number to act as an exchange for something that is worth the number on the paper. Even our accounts are just numbers. There is no value in them until we use it to exchange for something that holds actual value. The actual money that can be considered as assets are in the form of gold, silver, and other precious metal since they hold actual value themselves.

Modern cash or paper money is invented only for convenience. Having lots of cash is practically useless until you use it to exchange for something valuable. Else, when there is hyperinflation, the "value" of your money will decrease to the level that they are fit only as better toilet paper for your arse. Just look at the classic example of Germany before world war 2 or Zimbabwe. Trillions of dollars will only fetch you a loaf of bread.

Inflation, the currency's worst nightmare.

You can compare cash to water. Different currencies that existed in our world are just different flavoured water. Some might be more flavorful, delicious, and concentrated than the rest. Inflation occurs when there is too much money in circulation within the economy. When inflation happens, the water will be diluted heavily, losing its original taste and appeal and its "value" along the way.

Assets, on the other hand, allows the owners to own something valuable, rather than the worthless currencies. Owning stocks of companies means you actually own part of the company or business as one of the shareholders. In return for your support, you will receive part of the profits in the form of dividends. When you own properties, you will get returns from rentals or you will be able to get more money back if you sell it at a higher price than when you first purchased it.

Assets can be categorised into different types according to the degree of market liquidity of that asset. A higher degree of market liquidity means that one can buy or sell off the assets quicker in the market.

- High market liquidity - stocks
- Low market liquidity- properties

Properties are considered long term assets as it will slowly increase its value in time. Stocks on the other hand, might jump 300% in value if the company is bringing in a lot of profits, or having a very favourable business plan. However, stocks and other high liquitiy investments comes with certain risk factors.

It comes fast, it goes fast.

It is wise for one to have a mixture of assets with varying liquidity so that one can sell off the assets to resolve the cash flow issue.

Therefore, always remember that holding on to currencies or cash is the worst form of investment. It does not have value and is highly susceptible to manipulations and current economic conditions. One must focus on "cash flow" rather than "having a lot of cash" if one dreams of becoming rich.

The rich will always have enough cash flow to support their lifestyle, with the rest of the money stored in the form of assets that will increase in value and generate more money for them.

Therefore, you should save up enough money for emergencies, or enough to support your lifestyle if you lost your main income. Once you have secured your cash flow, you can embark on your investment journey and change the worthless currencies into something valuable.

"Learn from the rich to become rich."

ULTIMATE MONEY-MAKING MACHINE

Banks, the ultimate machine of making money

What is the best money-making machine in the world? Banks of course.

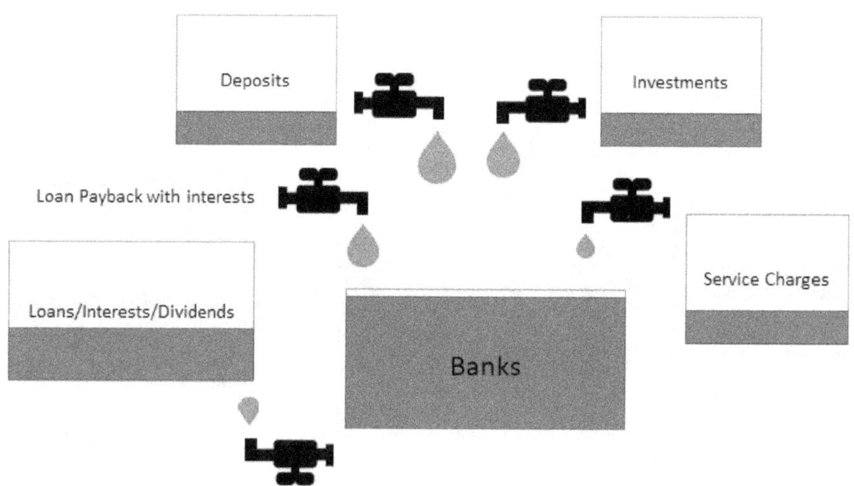

What business can be better than a bank? None. Its product is money! The very resource that everyone is trying to get!

Despite charging a small fee for the services that banks provide, such as money transfer, business account openings, etc, the income from it is actually negligent to the overall revenue. The main bulk of the revenue comes from the interest imposed on the loans taken by the borrowers. Banks actually earn around 10-18%, depending on the country and region for every loan given out.

Where do they get the money for all the loans? From you of course!

When someone opens a bank account and deposits the money, it is technically "owned" by the bank. You own nothing but just a number on your savings account. The bank will then use "your money" and lend it to someone that needs the money. The borrower will have to pay back the principal amount, along with the added interest to the amount. Banks feed on these interest returns as their main source of income for their expenses, operating costs, and "a bit of interest" for the deposit holders. Yes, saving accounts are actually a form of investment if you think of it, just very low returns but very safe nonetheless.

Let's do some calculations,

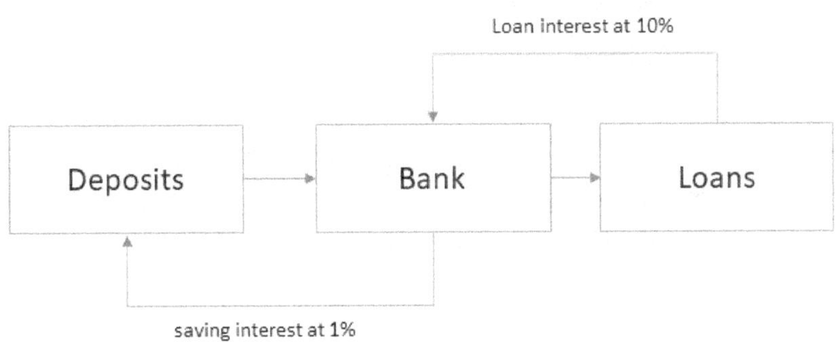

The bank will keep the 9% from the total money + interests paid back.

When the cycle repeats, the banks will have more money at hand, which they will diversify their portfolios to include bonds and stocks for more returns. Bigger banks will even loan out to governments, or providing consultancy services to get funding for the company or the government, which they would usually get a cut based on the final amount raised.

It is an ingenious business model. Using money to make more money. The bank does not need to set up any manufacturing facilities, secure the raw materials from its suppliers, renting warehouses to store its products, and managing its logistic costs. Its raw material, aka money, will be supplied consistently and willingly to them by the depositors. Its product, again, is a necessity and the most sort after "commodity" by all types of businesses, thereby saving tonnes of money in creating creative advertisements to attract customers. The only thing banks need to do to make their products more attractive is by setting lower interest rates for borrowing, and higher interest rates for saving your money.

What if there is a default?

Banks will usually perform background checks and risk analysis of an individual or an entity before deciding if they would want to loan the money to the borrowers. Everyone will be graded differently so that the banks can decide how much money can be given out. High risks borrowers usually get higher interest rates since the banks would want to recover as much money as possible before a default happens. When default did indeed happen, the banks will take ownership of the collaterals owned by the borrowers so that they could auction them off in the market to recover back the money in the event of a default.

How can a bank collapse?

The only way that a bank can collapse is when all the deposit holders decide to withdraw all their money from the bank, and all the borrowers actually default on their payment. The bank will have no reserve left to accommodate the withdrawal requests unless it starts to prints its own money, which is illegal unless it is the Federal Reserves. This scenario is highly unlikely but possible with the combination of mismanagement, disastrous economic conditions, and war.

If you are interested in the international banking business model, I suggest you to check out the history of the Medici or the Rothschild family.

HOW COMPANIES GET RICH?

How can a company become rich?

The company economy model runs similar to the individual economy model that we have discussed in the previous chapters. There are four key factors that company CEOs need to take note of if he or she wishes for the company to make loads of money:

- Brand Awareness
- Product Quality
- Market Share
- Cashflow

One of the best examples that adhere to these principles, and had set the example for others to follow is none other than Apple. Back then, it was a company that did badly and almost went out of business until Steve Jobs came and turn things around. Now the company itself is worth almost 2 trillion dollars and it is sitting on a huge pile of cash reserves. So, what makes it so successful?

Brand Awareness

Over the years, Apple had developed a distinct brand in its own right. When you talk about Apple, few things instantly came to mind: iPhone, iPad, MacBook, Mac OS, etc. They have succeeded in positioning themselves as a market leader in premium-quality lifestyle products. Their product lineup is so simple for anyone to remember and decide what they wanted. Though recently Apple's product lineup has added a bit more confusion, it is still leaner compared to other manufacturers like Samsung Xiaomi, Huawei, Lenovo, Dell, and so on. You will most likely be spending a significant time running through their product list. Just take a look at the number of smartphone models that Samsung has under them!

Leaner product lineups allow consumers to remember easily what your company offers and they can make quicker decisions when making a purchase.

Product Quality

Though there are some shortcomings and issues with their products, you can't deny that Apple products are of better quality than most of the products out there in the market. A lot of manufacturers eventually started copying the MacBook pro design for their own laptop lineups. Aluminium chassis is the norm now, replacing the usual cheap old plastic body that we used to love and hate at the same time. Hated the cheap feeling, but loved it for the durability and cost. I still remember that I could just throw my laptop around without worrying that I would cause a dent on the body frame.

When Apple is using the glass back design for the iPhone 4, most manufacturers followed suit. Why? Because Apple product's design is deemed to be premium and of better quality. This perception had been embedded deeply into the minds of consumers out there. Therefore, the quickest way to improve the brand's perception would be copying the designs of those successful products.

Consumers will buy good quality products even when there is less marketing done, as long as the brand awareness is there. What Apple has done to their brand is to embed the thought that Apple product users are fashionable, high class, rich, and successful. Everyone would want to be seen holding an iPhone or using a MacBook in the cafes. Using an Android device is deemed to be of a lower class or a nerd. In fact, Apple has done so well that now it has achieved cult status for its products and brand name.

Apple knows how to market their products without excessive marketing. Marketing is in fact a double edge sword. It costs a lot for a company and it might not yield the result anticipated. When a product is over-marketed, and the end product quality is bad or a disappointment, then it will have an adverse effect on the company's brand and example. Just look at the failure of Samsung's Note 7. The company will always be remembered for creating a smartphone that might explode on your face.

Market Share

Apple products are sold worldwide. You can find an Apple store or it's distribution channel in almost every major city in the world. Bill Gates once said that his goal is to put a PC on every desk. But in fact, it was Steve Jobs that first popularise the personal PC with a usable graphic interface through Apple Lisa. The compact size and unique user interface experience has made the product much more accessible to the public. Apple then follows up with another product that is more widely known, the Macintosh. Though recently Apple was dethroned from the smartphone market, they still command significant market share.

Why market share is important?

You can think of the market share as a pool of resources and everyone is trying to get as many resources as possible for themselves. The only way to get hold of that resources is to get people into buying their products so that more profits can be generated. That is why companies are trying all sorts of methods to outflank their competitors to gain more market share for their products and services.

The bigger the market share they hold, the more money they will get.

Cashflow

This is just the simple math discussed earlier. You will need to price your product carefully so that your product price is still affordable for your target audience, and able to generate some profit from it. The extra cash will come in handy during rainy times, as well as to support your business expansion.

Key math for any businesses:

Sales amount - expenses + costs = profit

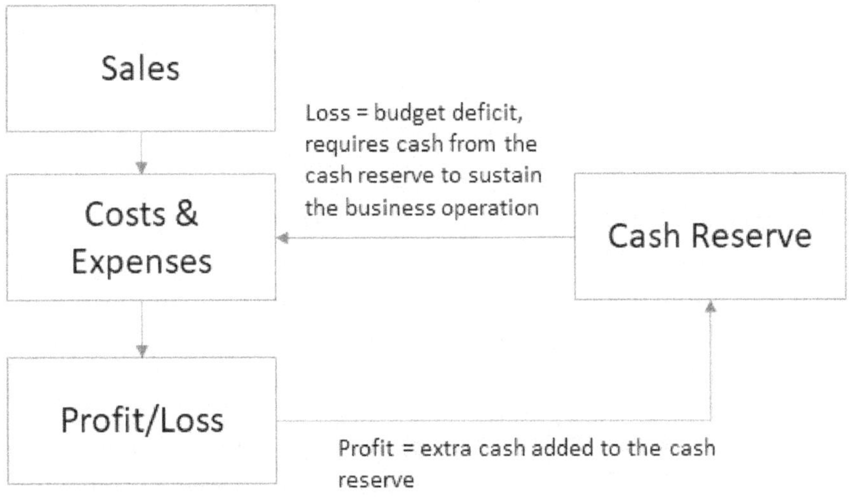

With the tremendous amount of profit generated from the hardware sales, Apple has the extra cash to invest in other businesses.

Recently, the company has unveiled a slew of new services, e.g. Apple TV, Apple Music, Apple Books, Apple Pay, etc. These services added to the already increasing revenue growth of the App Store.

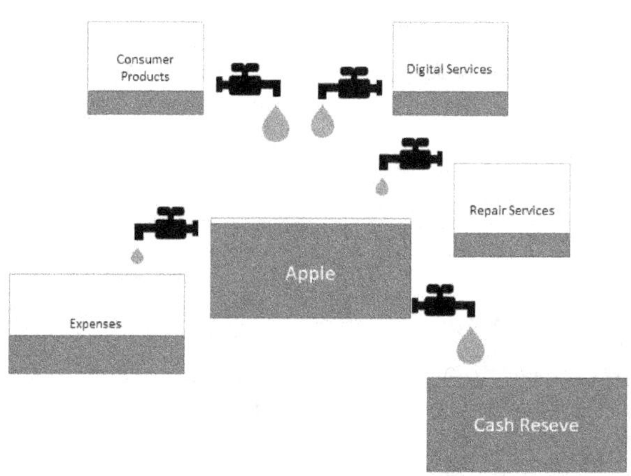

One more thing,

Always monitor the expenditure of the company

A lot of companies tend to overlook the expenditure until the amount became too huge when sales are down. The management had installed a bigger water tap to allow a bigger outflow of money, aka spending.

When the profit from the sales is unable to sustain the company's spending, the management will rush to cut down the company expenses drastically, e.g. staff layoffs and retrenchments, allowances, salary cuts, etc, in order to keep the business afloat. The ones that usually got affected most are the bunch at the lowest level in a pyramid hierarchy. This group of people is also the most susceptible to the negative effect of an economic slowdown since their small income, as compared to the high salaries of those in the top management, would leave them with little savings to ride through an economic storm.

Remember the water tank model?

This sudden measure will have a huge negative impact on the economy as a whole. Those staff who relied on the company as their main source, or the only source of income, will be greatly affected when they are being laid off. Their water tanks will soon be dried up if they are unable to get another job or income soon. The family members who relied on the breadwinner of the house will find them in a desperate situation as each of them will not be able to receive the resources from their only source to sustain their lives. Multiply by the hundreds or thousands of people losing the jobs, you will soon find the country's economy in a dire situation as more businesses started to close down.

The water flow will stop, the same goes for economic activities.

What can be done?

Most companies I find tend to overspend the profit from the business on the fat pay checks for their management team, expanding the team or business too aggressively, and invest in risky businesses with the hope of getting more money back. The remaining crumbs will then trickle down to the staff as their annual bonus or increments. The expenditure grows exponentially with an increase in profit.

Set aside a percentage of the profit into the company's emergency fund.

The emergency cash fund can serve as a temporary backup when the company runs into a deficit when it is not doing well. The company can also allocate some of the money in safer investments that could guarantee healthy returns to grow the emergency fund further.

Start to automate the business or back-office operations

This will allow companies to scale their businesses without the need to hire more staff to do the job. This would help the company to save some money on the retirement fund, insurance, allowance, bonus payouts for the extra staff that needs to be hired during the business expansion. When the economy slows down, the company will not have to lay off the people and pay out huge compensations to them.

Review the expenditure regularly

Companies should establish a committee to review the expenditure on a monthly or quarterly basis, in which the committee can decide how the money can be channeled more effectively to the departments that are vital for the company's business activities and expansion plan.

Companies should also consider selling online

In this digital era, companies should focus on creating an online presence and start selling their products and services online. More and more mobile users are using their mobile phones to buy online. Chat services like WhatsApp are even introducing the feature for consumers to purchase a product from the seller through the messaging service. By setting up or joining an e-commerce platform, the company will be able to utilise the power of technology, not just another sales channel, they could personalise the buying experience for their customers. Loyalty programmes with rewards is one way to retain customers. Apart from that, going digital means saving costs on marketing as new products can be automatically sent to the customers' email or mobile app. The company can also use the data gathered from customer feedback and product popularity to further improve on the product quality, offerings, and pricing.

Borrowing to expand the business, is it a good thing?

A lot of companies are actually taking out loans to expand their businesses. I wouldn't recommend it unless the business investment is almost certainly profitable, and the company can easily pay back the loans along with the high interest charged. For some, it might provide temporary relief to their cashflow woes under difficult circumstances. But I have seen more and more companies are borrowing money to inflate the company value. This usually creates an illusion for investors that the company is doing very well and business is expanding rapidly. What they didn't realise is that the company might end up with a huge debt when the loans matured. The original owners might have cashed out, leaving those poor, small-time investors defenseless, which they would probably lose all their money from investing in such a company.

Therefore, borrowing is never really a good thing unless the benefit outweighs the cons. It is vital to always ensure that the company set aside extra cash during good times so that the cash can be used to cushion out any negative impact during difficult times. There are many cases where the owners of a successful company splashed out on fancy sports cars, ultra-luxury office renovations, and other wastage, only to find the company saddled in huge debt when times are bad.

Only borrow if all alternatives are exhausted.

HOW COUNTRIES GET RICH?

A country runs significantly different and a lot more complicated than a company. The company only has a handful of stakeholders to please, and their main focus is profitability. A country, on the other hand, needs to take care of all its citizens: rich, poor, old, young. The government of the country has the obligation and responsibility to ensure that all the citizens are free from extreme poverty and their basic needs like food, shelter, medical, and others are addressed. Unlike a company where they just need to make sure that the company generates enough profit to pay the salary of its staff. If it is unable to do so, the company will just let go of its staff. A country, on the other hand, is unable to just kill off its citizens like that, unless you are Stalin or Hitler.

In countries that practice democracy, their citizens are effectively the shareholders of the country. The government acting as the management team of the country has the responsibility to improve the lives of its people. And doing so will require a huge amount of money. Think of it like the parent taking care of millions of children, your child care bills will already be sky-high, and you still need to fork out more for other expenses for their education, medical bills, and so on.

So where do countries get their money from?

Taxes

This is the main source of revenue for any country in the world. The government of the day will collect various forms of taxes, e.g. personal income tax, corporate tax, import duty, property tax, road tax, and many more. All these monies collected will be used for the government's operation expenditure and development projects for the betterment of the country and its citizens. The head of government will usually present a budget specifying how the tax money will be used in the parliament every year. Failing to pass the budget will cause severe disruption to the country as the government will not be able to run without the funds. Once the budget is passed, the funds will be allocated to the respective agencies to carry out the work according to the plan.

Investments

Some countries like Singapore and the United Arab Emirates (UAE) are well known for establishing entities identified as Sovereign Wealth Fund using the extra cash in the coffers to invest in businesses to generate more returns for the country. These Sovereign Wealth Funds are effectively the business and investment arm of the country. Such funds are crucial for countries with limited or no natural resources, e.g. Singapore, or countries that are over-reliant on one commodity such as petroleum. If anything happens to their main source of income, these funds would be able to provide a desperately needed lifeline.

How can a country become rich?

Just like the individual or the corporate model, a country needs to set up multiple sources of income to increase its coffer for development projects that will lead to the betterment of its citizens. As pointed out above, the two main sources of income are taxes and investments, where the former is the main income.

If a country requires more money to operate, the easiest and quickest way would be to increase the tax rate. However, doing so will increase the burden of the citizens and might ultimately lead to civil unrest if the rate is stupidly high.

So, what can the country do besides increasing the tax rates of individuals and businesses?

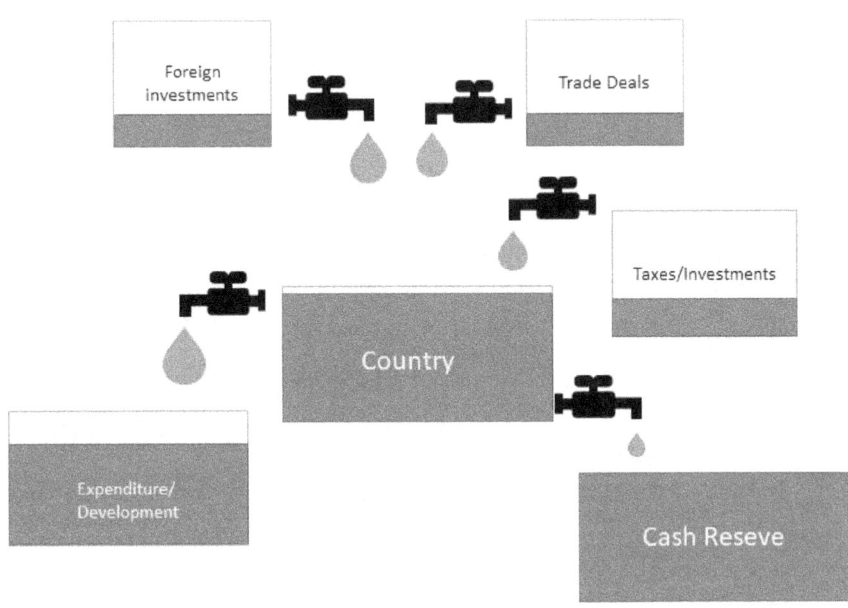

Increase the inflow of foreign money

Getting money from other countries will allow more money to be circulated within the economy of a country. There are a few ways to do so:

- Tourism

If the country has a unique culture, an awesome variety of food, and scenic attractions, it will be a great opportunity to develop these sectors into major tourist attractions. When tourists come for visits, they will bring in money to be spent on local businesses. As businesses thrive, so will the tax income.

- Direct Foreign Investments

The government should establish policies that are business-friendly for foreign companies to set up their business operations within the country, e.g. favourable terms, tax incentives, etc. When foreign companies set up operations within the country, it means that they will be bringing in a lot of foreign capital into the country for property rentals, staff hiring, equipment purchases from local suppliers, and many more.

Hire Local First Policy

The government should encourage local and foreign businesses to hire local talents instead of foreign workers. When a country has too many foreign workers, there will be a greater outflow of money that was meant for the local economy since these workers will be sending a good portion of their net salary back to their home country. The "Hire local first policy" will also help to reduce unemployment rates in the country, bringing jobs and money to the citizens which in return will generate more income, via tax for the national coffer.

Becomes a Net Exporter

The government should focus on making the country a net exporter, meaning the country will export more goods than importing them. By becoming a net exporter, the country can generate extra income from taxes when businesses are selling for other countries, thereby earning money from foreign countries. It also means that the country has enough resources to sustain its population. The exports can be in the form of physical goods, services, and talents.

Increase income taxes gradually

When a country has more money circulating in its economy, either via businesses, foreign investments, tourism, returns of investments, etc, the government can gradually increase the tax rate for the income of businesses and individuals. This will not increase the burden much as there is enough money lying around. Furthermore, it could help manage inflation in the country. The government can then spend it on development projects, or inject more capital onto its investments and let the cycle repeat.

Investments in strategic sectors

The government can invest in key sectors that will guarantee returns. Some of the key sectors include energy, telecommunications, and banking. The dividend payout from these investments could then be channeled back to the economy. The government should be very careful in selecting the investment portfolios to avoid investing in risky sectors which might end up losing all the taxpayers' money.

Cut down government operation expenditure

The government should start leveraging on the power of technology to automate the back-office operations of government agencies. This will allow the government to maintain a lean workforce, yet a highly efficient one. The government could save up money on pensions and payouts for the extra staff that needs to be supported, thus preventing a massive burn to the coffer. This will also prevent the civil service from being over-bloated, and more people could be placed in the private sector. This would also mean that more people will be out there to contribute to the country's economy, either working in the private companies or setting up their own businesses, and not sucking the nation's coffer dry. However, in countries that are practising "flawed" democracy, the civil servants usually became the "hostage" to the government where they will be forced to "vote" for the government during the elections or they might end up losing their job. The bigger the civil force, the more votes the government will get.

However, in order to have a huge support base, the government will hire as many people as possible, with some even establishing agencies that basically does nothing or very little work, all just to secure the votes from them. Such setup will quickly drain the nation's coffer dry as we will see

Expenses > income (from taxes)

What happens when a country runs out of money?

When a country is proposing a deficit budget, meaning that the government is spending more money than its income, the government will need to find other sources to cover the deficits. Depending on the country's laws, the government could tap into its cash reserve or borrow from financial institutions to fund the deficit.

As we have learnt before, taking out a loan is never a good thing due to the high-interest rates imposed. When the government is having budget deficits every year, it will soon balloon into a massive debt. Most countries realized this, and they have imposed something knowns as the debt ceiling to prevent the government of the day from borrowing more money. However, on most occasions, the senators or members of parliament will just vote to increase the debt ceiling. When a country is unable to service its debts, it is effectively declared bankrupt. This was what happened to Greece a couple of years back.

What happens next?

If a country is unable to service its debts, creditors will have the right to take over the country's assets and resources as a form of payment. When Germany lost World War 1, it is required to pay a huge amount of indemnification to the allied countries that won the war. The coffers ran dry, causing severe economic depression to the Germans. After failing to pay for the reparations set under the Treaty of Versailles, the French just sent in its armies and occupied the Ruhr area of Germany, in order to extract its resources as the payment owed to them.

Once the country's assets or resources are taken over by the creditors, the country can be considered "colonised" in some form.

The country will no longer be able to assert control of the assets or resources unless the government took them back by force, thereby risking war with the country where the creditors reside. This is also the very reason why certain countries are wary of the "belt and road" initiative by the Chinese government. Once they fell into the debt trap, the future of their nation will be at the mercy of the creditors.

MONETERISM

The concept of "Monetarism" states that the supply of money is one of the key drivers of economic growth as depicted with the diagram illustrated in the Water Tank setup.

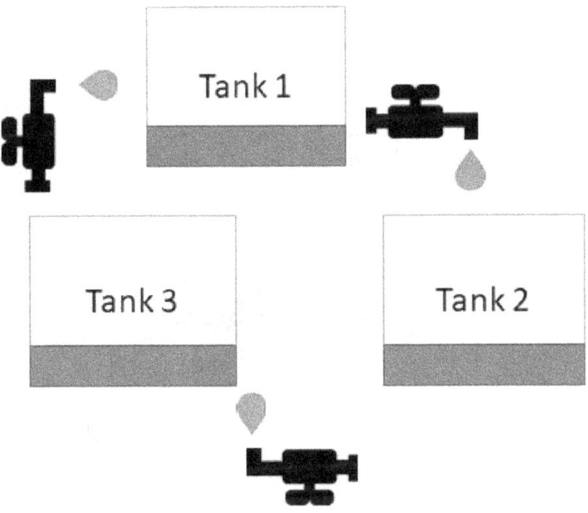

But is having too much money a good thing?

Not really.

Having too much money in the economy will lead to inflation where the price of goods will be driven up since there is now more money lying around in the average consumer's pocket. Imagine there is a sudden influx of water into the water system, some of the tanks might overflow. The rest of the tanks will start to demand bigger cuts from the full tank, hoping to fill up their own tank. If all the greedy tanks started demanding more water from tanks and changed their traps to allow a bigger flow of water (higher price), what would become of the setup when the water source is depleted?

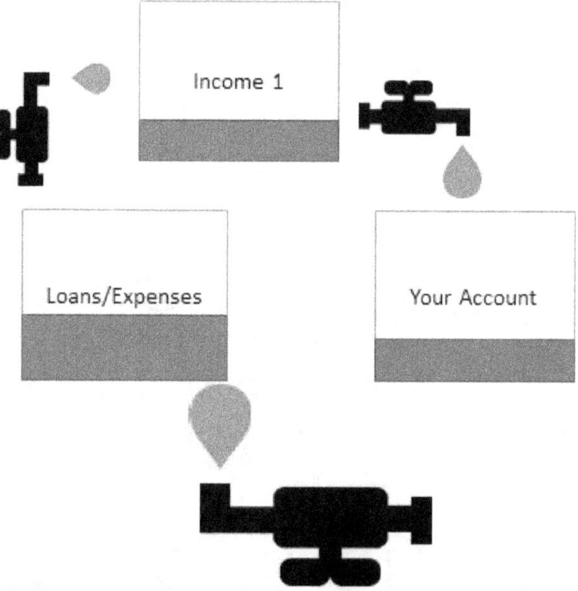

Our outflowing water tap will be bigger if we increase spending when we have extra money lying around.

We will see the same case as follows:

In a normal situation,

$$Income - expenses = balance$$

We have the income that is enough to pay for the expenses of our basic needs and leave some balance for savings.

Good times - positive economic growth,

More income- more expenses with utilise/rental increased = balance

Our income increased during the explosive economic growth in the country, allowing us to purchase more things, or move to a better residential unit. During this time, we are still able to save up some money from the balance after deducting all our expenditure.

Bad times - negative economic growth,

Less income - more expenses with utilise/rental increased = deficit (negative balance)

When the economy crashed, our income decreased significantly due to pay cuts or job loss. However, our expenditure will remain the same as we have signed the rental contract when we move to a better unit. Now our income is not sufficient to pay off the expenses incurred, leaving us with a deficit where we will need to use the savings to cover the extra amount.

Note: Provided that the person still wishes to maintain the same lifestyle and businesses are not reducing the price of goods.

The same economic woes will be repeated. When businesses run out of money again, they will have to start cutting jobs. The government will have to step in yet again to pump in more money to rescue the economy. It will be a vicious cycle all over again. Continuously pouring money into the economy is not the solution to our economic issues. Worse off if the government had to resort to borrowings to get the money required.

What can be done?

The problem lies with our monetary system. Money nowadays doesn't carry any values. It is just a number to indicate the value of a certain item or work performed. Back then, money does have a value itself, which usually are in the form of precious metals like gold or silver. Since the previous are very limited in amount, they are used for big purchases. The normal peasants usually trade using goods in the form of a barter system since the precious metals are hard to come by. All the gold and silver coins are reserved for the lords of the lands and the king.

Old Money vs Modern Currency

Old days when money has value

Ten sack of rice (equal value) = a piece of gold
Castle = a hundred pieces of gold

Goods (after determining the value) = exchange with = other goods (of equal value)

One piece of gold will be as valuable as ten sacks of rice. Gold itself has value because it is an item that can be traded as a form of goods, like raw materials for gold jewellery pieces.

Modern currency

Goods (after determining the value) = buy with currency with some numbers to indicate the value

Modern currency itself is worthless. It is either a number in your account or a piece of paper that costs pennies to print. It can not be traded as a form of goods like gold. It does not hold any value at all. All it does is to represent an arbitrary number for you to make purchases.

Gold, silver, and other precious metals have a finite amount. It would be very difficult to flood the economy with a massive influx of gold or silver. This prevented inflation from happening. As the resource is depleted, the value of the precious metal will go up.

Modern currencies on the other hand can be printed or created out of thin air. The resource is infinite. When the country needs money for the economy, the Federal Reserve will just print more money. This means the common taxpayers will have to fork out more money to pay for the debts owed for the extra money created. To put in bluntly, our modern currency does not hold value, but is associated with debt. The money that we hold are actually the debt of another person. Remember that banks take our money and lend it to those applied for bank loans? So in conclusion, modern currency is worth nothing.

Put together a positive and a negative figure together and you get 0.

However, that will be a separate topic on its own.

Back to inflation

So what can governments do to minimise the impact of inflation?

- Increase the interest rates for loans so that fewer people would borrow and add more money into the economy

- Increase the income tax rates to cut consumer spending, thereby reducing the money flow into the economy.

- Price control on goods and services to prevent the drastic increase in price that will allow more money circulation.

- Prevent the economy from growing too fast too soon. The growth rate should be consistent with the population growth as well as the supply and demand trend. When the demand outpaces supply, the price of goods will increase.

"*Pumping money into the economy is akin to pumping air into a balloon, it will just explode sooner or later.*"

"*Circulating goods with value will strengthen the economy like vitamins to the body.*"

CORRUPTION IS THE CANCER TO A COUNTRY'S ECONOMY

The money within the country's economy should be circulating freely within so everyone will be able to reap the benefits. But humans are born to sin, with the ability to commit heinous crimes due to greed. When the corruption level is high, it will have a detrimental effect on the country's economy.

Why is that?

When corruption happens, usually in the form of bribery and monies are channeled into slush funds owned by corrupt politicians. This form of money is usually hidden from public scrutiny, and most likely at a foreign bank account.

Corrupted politicians are robbing the country like a robber robbing the bank, the only difference is robbers will get charged and sent to jail, politicians will often remain in power and escape justice.

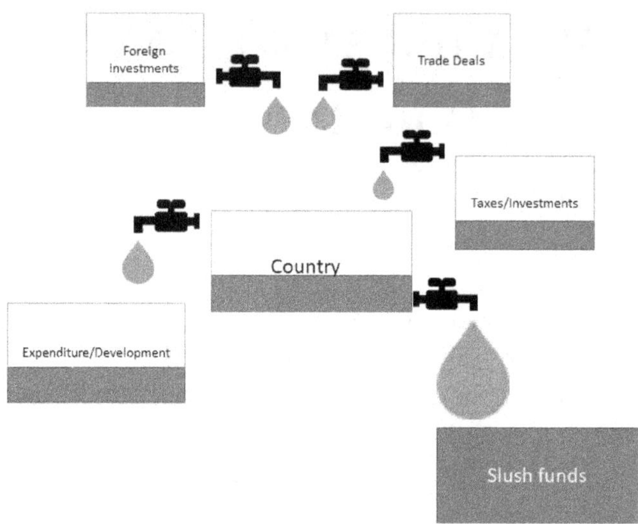

This will cause the country's economy to quickly run out of money. Through the economic model above, we know that a country needs to have more money circulating within the economy and not sending it out. By doing so, they would be causing disruption to an otherwise healthy economy. Money kept flowing out to their secret bank accounts. When there is not enough money in the economy, we will begin to see some of the tanks drying up.

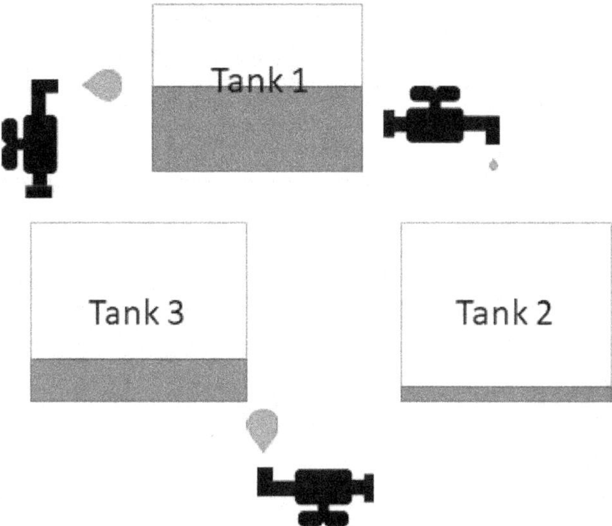

When it does, it will pose risks to individuals and companies that rely on the water from that tank. This will cause a domino effect when one dried-up tank is unable to supply the water to the next tank. The nation will plunge into more troubles (as discussed in the chapter earlier) as the government starts to borrow more money.

The corrupted politicians will be oblivious to the suffering of the people since their own tank is still overflowing with the water stolen from the people!

So if you want to be rich and have more money, your chances are better with a transparent and corrupt-free government.

GLOBAL PANDEMIC, THE BANE OF ECONOMY

Any plague spreads fastest at the heart of the economic activities, e.g. at the market where merchants and customers are gathered in a small, packed area to conduct trading. The highly contagious bacteria or virus can be transmitted easily when the goods that are already exposed or contaminated by the pathogen, exchanged hands between the buyer and seller. Furthermore, if it is an airborne disease, one will be infected by just being at the location for some time.

To stop the infections from spreading would mean restricting or completely preventing any forms of interactions between people. This is the most effective method yet to control the spreading of a plague that has no known cure or vaccine.

If the candles are chained together in a tight formation, the flame from the adjacent candle will spread to the next wick. It won't take long before all the candles are lit up.

If the lit candles are separated and isolated, the remaining candles
will be safe from being lit up by the flame since the next candle
will be too far apart for the flame from the previous candle to be
spread to the wick. After some time, the flame on the last lit candle
will die off, thus eradicating the chances for other candles to be lit
up.

That is why most of the governments in the world imposed some
level of lockdowns and restrictions on economic activities to
prevent the spread of the plague. This, in turn, causes a devastating
effect on the country's economy as the flow of money will be
disrupted. No interactions mean no tradings, and no tradings mean
no economic activities, thus no flow of money around. Even with
the advancement of technology where goods can be traded online,
there are still sectors that will be severely affected, e.g. tourism,
airline, and service oriented industries. These sectors employ a
great number of workers. When the lockdowns are in place, the
companies under the aforementioned industries would lose sales
and businesses, which would turn to cut jobs and salaries of their
staff in order to save up some cash. The staff members who were
let go will find themselves unable to spend like they are used to,
hence tightening the flow of money from this group of people to
other industries.

Apart from that, infected patients might have to spend more on
healthcare and hospital bills. If more people are infected, it will tilt

the balance of the flow of money where most of them will be
channeled to only essential services. Since more money is spent on
medical, it leaves little for them to spend their money elsewhere.
The little remaining money they have will be saved for additional
medical bills if the illness prolongs. Others who are not infected
will be too scared to go out and spend their money at restaurants or
the malls, thereby reducing the economic activities and thus
stopping the flow of money to the businesses.

Such a change would leave a country in a balancing act. The
country needs to prevent more people from dying from the
infection since they need all able-bodied and healthy individuals to
engage in economic activities. But at the same time, they need
economic activities to keep the money flowing. The quickest
solution would be pumping more money to those affected
industries to help them stay afloat, at least for the time being. But
pouring more money too fast, too soon will lead to inflation and
widen the gap in income inequality.

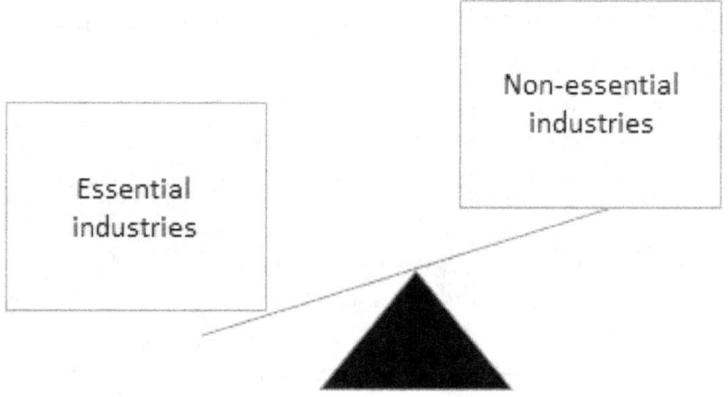

Why can't the companies that are earning help the economy?

Companies benefitting from the situation will unlikely be
expanding their operations and team since it will be a risk to them
if the whole plague situation dies out unless the situation is a

permanent one. They might end up having to spend more on salaries in a bloated organisation, which will lead to another round of layoffs later on when the plague subsided.

What are the alternatives?

In order to mitigate the risk, governments could initiate temporary policies as follows:

- Increase the taxes for those industries, companies, or individuals that are getting reaping the benefits from the situation, e.g. masks providers, hand sanitiser suppliers, etc. The extra money collected can be channeled back to those industries in need.

- Negotiate with the banks to temporarily reduce the interest rates to reduce the burden of the borrowers so that they could avoid defaulting the payment. For companies or individuals who are most affected by the situation, moratoriums can be considered as a temporary relief. Lower interest rates would also encourage some companies to take up loans to resolve their cash flow issues.

- Zero tax or a reduced rate if the non-essential goods are purchase online. This would encourage more consumers to purchase non-essential items through e-commerce platforms to ensure the continuation and survival of the businesses. The zero-tax rate will be very tempting for consumers as they would be able to save up a sizeable amount when they perform bulk purchases.

- Hefty fines for individuals or companies that deliberately increase infection within a community, such as not getting treatment or isolate oneself after tested positive for the infection. This is to create awareness about an individual's responsibility to the community and to instil discipline to the public, as well as preventing the infection rate from spiralling out of control. The fines can then be used to assist those in need.

- Assist businesses that are badly affected to contribute in some way, e.g. engage airline companies to assist in the logistic segments, temporarily convert the workers in the tourism sector to assist the government initiatives to spread awareness about the disease and to help out the overstretched medical team at hospitals.

The policies should be aimed at ensuring enough money flows across all sectors. The setup might have changed, but the flow of money should continue to reach all the individuals within the economic model in order for the model to sustain. Just like the balanced water tank setup.

Ultimately, it requires all of us to be disciplined and take up our community responsibilities. If you or the person you know is sick, please isolate or seek medical attention immediately and avoid interactions with other people in a crowded area. If all of us can abide by the rule, we would be able to control the disease outbreak better and avoid major disruption to our economy.

FINAL WORD

The flow of money forms the basis of any economic model through supply and demand. However, one must always be observant as a tiny bit of disruption to the flow; or the supply and demand, might either bring wealth, or chaos on different levels.

So, with the information in this book, I hope you are able to utilise it in your life seek out your water sources and get more water today!

Recommended Reading(s):

1. *Layman's Guide to Investing, with a bit of common sense (2020)*, by Kyle C

Other books by this Author:

1. *Words for Humanity (2020)*, by Kyle C

www.ingramcontent.com/pod-product-compliance
Lightning Source LLC
Chambersburg PA
CBHW061312140726
47998CB00006B/2364